This book should be returned to any branch of the Lancashire County Library on or before the date shown

01/04/10

EBL

BURNLEY CAMPUS
01282 682273

- 5 DEC 2011

2 7 OCT 2015

- 7 DEC 2019

Lancashire County Library
Bowran Street
Preston PR1 2UX

w

es

LL1(A)

SPIRIT OF
LANCASHIRE

JON SPARKS

First published in Great Britain in 2007, reprinted 2009

Copyright text and photographs © 2007 Jon Sparks.

British Library Cataloguing-in-Publication Data
A CIP record for this title is available from the Br

ISBN 978 1 906887 48 3

PiXZ Books

Halsgrove House, Ryelands Industrial Estate,
Bagley Road, Wellington, Somerset TA21 9PZ
Tel: 01823 653777
Fax: 01823 216796
email: sales@halsgrove.com

An imprint of Halstar Ltd, part of the Halsgrove
Information on all Halsgrove titles is available at: www.halsgrove.com

Printed and bound by Grafiche Flaminia, Italy

Introduction

To distil the diversity of Lancashire into a sentence or two is manifestly impossible. Most of the industrial towns are concentrated in a narrow band along the margins of the uplands, where abundant water-power drove the early stages of the Industrial Revolution before the coming of steam. The lowlands of the west, previously wet and inhospitable, were progressively drained and turned into farmland to feed the growing towns. For the workers in those towns life was undeniably grim, but freedom and clean air were found in a Sunday walk out onto the moors, and perhaps a week at one of the new resorts along the coast.

The valley of the Ribble, Lancashire's major river, cuts the eastern upland into two major blocks, the West Pennines to the south and the Forest of Bowland to the north. Bowland, much more lightly impacted by industry, is bounded in turn on its northern flank by the Lune valley. The landscape of the Ribble and Lune valleys is lightyears away from the stereotype of Lancashire. Instead it is what many people think of as quintessentially English: a rumpled patchwork of green fields, hedgerows and woods, a scene that is all but extinct in large parts of southern England.

Wyresdale and the Bowland Fells
The Bowland Fells form a substantial block of high ground in the
north of the county, reaching to within 10 kilometres of the coast.

River Lune near Loyn Bridge

The Lune is the most northerly of Lancashire's major rivers and the Lune valley has some of the county's loveliest scenery.

Fallow deer, Thrang Moss

Opposite page:
Littledale and Ward's Stone from Baines Crag
Baines Crag is only a few kilometres from Lancaster,
on the edge of the Forest of Bowland AONB.   On the skyline
is Ward's Stone, the highest point in the Bowland Fells.

Channels, Morecambe Bay, from Warton Crag
Low tide reveals the Bay's eternally shifting maze of channels and mud-flats.

Sunset from Jack Scout, Silverdale

The cliffs of Jack Scout overlook the meeting of the Kent Estuary and Morecambe Bay,
beyond which are Grange-over-Sands and the ridge of Hampsfell.

**Evening,
Heysham Head**

Late evening light warms
the wave-worn rocks
of Heysham Head,
on the edge of
Morecambe Bay.

Opposite page:
**View from Jeffrey Hill,
Longridge Fell**

Longridge Fell is a
single ridge rising to
350m and standing alone
with no connection to
other high ground, though
geologically it is part of
the Forest of Bowland.

Cockersand Abbey

This is just about all that remains of Cockersand Abbey,
overlooking the mouth of the River Lune.

Warton church, stars and stripes
Warton, just north of Carnforth, is an attractive village, but there's a specific reason why it draws many American visitors. St Oswald's church has connections with the ancestors of George Washington, the first president of the US.

Paraglider, Jeffrey Hill
Jeffrey Hill is one of Lancashire's finest viewpoints, at least among those easily accessible by road.

Opposite page:
The Hodder valley and Whitendale from Hall Hill
This is not just the heart of the Forest of Bowland, but the heart of the United Kingdom: the tiny village of Dunsop Bridge, partly visible in the middle of the picture, is often stated to be the geographical centre of the UK.

Fireworks over the River Lune and Castle Hill, Lancaster

Lancaster's Castle Hill is the regular venue for a major fireworks display on the Saturday nearest to 5 November.

Opposite page:
Kitcham Hill

Evening on Grit Fell
Grit Fell is on the main northern ridge of the Bowland Fells
and is fairly easily reached from the road at Jubilee Tower.

Downham and Pendle Hill

Downham is one of the showpiece
villages of the Ribble valley.

Troy Quarry, near Haslingden
One usually thinks of the Millstone Grit as being grey or even black, but unweathered rock can be remarkably colourful.

Opposite page:
Walkers at Dunsop Head
Before the Right to Roam, the track over Dunsop Head was one of a small number of legal routes over the high ridges of Bowland.

21

India Mill, Darwen

India Mill, and specifically its chimney, dominates the small town of Darwen. Dating from the 1860s, the chimney is 92m (just over 300 ft) high.

Darwen Tower and the Bowland Fells
Construction of the tower began in 1897, marking Queen
Victoria's Diamond Jubilee as well as access to the moors.

Leck Beck
This is the very edge of Lancashire – the boundary follows the beck – and the most northerly location in the book.

Opposite page:
Harvest patterns, Quernmore
The Quernmore valley lies just east of Lancaster.

The Old Pier, St Anne's-on-Sea

St Anne's-on-Sea is usually called simply St Anne's, and is often considered part of a single town with neighbouring Lytham. These are the remains of a

Infirmary Street, Blackburn

Terraced housing is part of the stereotype picture of Lancashire,
but there is a lot less than there was, say, fifty years ago.

Stonyhurst

Stonyhurst College was formerly home to the Shireburn family. Today it is one of the country's leading Catholic boarding schools.

Opposite page:
Climber at Trowbarrow

The limestone quarry at Trowbarrow doubles as a nature reserve and an important climbing venue.

29

St George's Quay, Lancaster
The eighteenth century waterfront remains largely intact,
though the former warehouses have been converted to residential use.

Opposite page:
Reservoir at Roddlesworth

Quernmore valley and Clougha Pike

Angler, Halton-on-Lune
Halton lies just a short distance upstream from the city of Lancaster.
The River Lune is highly rated by anglers, notably for its salmon, but also for coarse fishing.

Oak tree, Bleasdale
The low hill on the horizon is Beacon Fell, now a
country park, especially popular with Preston folk.

Opposite page:
Lighthouse in the Lune Estuary
This little lighthouse still guards the mouth of the
River Lune and is an important navigational aid for vessels
heading to Glasson Dock or upstream to Lancaster.

Low tide, Morecambe Bay

The viewpoint here is about a hundred metres off the promenade at Bare.

Morecambe Bay from Warton Crag
It's not often, these days, that you get decent snow cover right down to sea level.

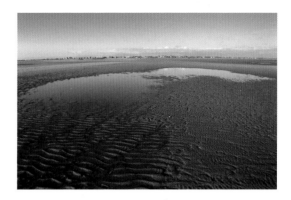

St Anne's Sands

The vast extent of the sands at St Anne's
becomes apparent in this view.

Opposite page:
Evening, Procter Moss

Procter Moss is on a low ridge above the
village of Dolphinholme, in Wyresdale.

Riversway Marina, Preston

Preston became a recognised seaport in 1843 and the docks officially closed in 1981.

Opposite page:
Blackpool Tower and illuminations

Blackpool has been staging its illuminations, with interruptions only
for two world wars, since 1912. Today the illuminations stretch
almost ten kilometres from Starr Gate to Bispham.

The Windmill, Lytham

Windmills were once common in lowland Lancashire, where water power was unavailable. This is the best-known survivor, and Lytham's principal landmark. It is prominently placed on Lytham Green, right by the shore.

Opposite page:
Crook O'Lune

Crook O'Lune is about 5km (3 miles) east of Lancaster, where the river makes a sharp bend through a natural rocky barrier.

Anglers, Stone Jetty, Morecambe

Rawtenstall, snow

Rawtenstall lies at the heart of the Rossendale valley. Its most singular claim to fame is that it's home to Britain's last surviving Temperance Bar, also described as 'The Pub with No Beer', in Fitzpatrick's Herbal Health Shop.

Halton-on-Lune
A crisp winter's day, with the River Lune partially frozen.
The tower of St Wilfrid's church is on the left of the picture.

Opposite page:
Moon over Wyresdale

Accrington roofscape

This landscape of terraced houses and factory chimneys is probably
what many unenlightened Southerners think of as typically Lancashire.

Showers over the Fylde

This view gives a good impression of the flatness of the Fylde, and indeed
most of western Lancashire. It also helps to explain why Blackpool Tower –
right of centre – is such a prominent landmark from so many viewpoints.

West Lancashire from Parbold Hill
This view is taken from the footpath between High Moor and Parbold Beacon.

The Ashton Memorial and Morecambe Bay

To travellers on the M6, Lancaster's Ashton Memorial is a familiar sight.

Longridge Fell from Bashall Eaves

Opposite page:
Rainbow over Clougha Pike

Dean Black Brook

Dean Black Brook cuts through the edge of the moors above White Coppice.

Morecambe Bay from Heysham Head

The ruins of a tiny chapel are said to mark the spot
where St Patrick first set foot in England.

Hawes Water

Hawes Water (not to be confused with the much larger lake
of the same name in Cumbria) lies near Silverdale.

Viaduct, Wayoh Reservoir
The well-watered West Pennine uplands are ringed with
reservoirs constructed to supply water to nearby towns and cities.

Warton Crag and Carnforth

Opposite page:
Banks Marsh

Autumn in the Hindburn valley

The Harris Museum and Art Gallery, Preston

Usually called simply 'the Harris', this Grade I listed building stands in the heart of Preston.

Bolton-by-Bowland

Bolton-by-Bowland, in the Ribble valley, is a well-preserved village
and has the unusual distinction of having two village greens.

Opposite page:
Backwater near Higher Broomfield

This scene is just a short stroll from Arkholme, in the heart of the Lune valley.

Eric Morecambe statue, Morecambe Promenade